Mark McGwire

Additional Titles in the Sports Reports Series

Mark McGwire

Star Home Run Hitter

Stew Thornley

 Enslow Publishers, Inc.

40 Industrial Road	PO Box 38
Box 398	Aldershot
Berkeley Heights, NJ 07922	Hants GU12 6BP
USA	UK

http://www.enslow.com

Library of Congress Cataloging-in-Publication Data

Thornley, Stew.
     Mark McGwire: star home run hitter / Stew Thornley.
        p. cm. — (Sports reports)
     Includes bibliographical references (p.) and index.
     Summary: Examines the life and career of baseball superstar Mark McGwire,
from his earliest playing days to his record-breaking 1998 season.
     ISBN 0-7660-1329-4
     1. McGwire, Mark, 1963– —Juvenile literature. 2. Baseball players—United
States—Biography—Juvenile literature. [1. McGwire, Mark, 1963– . 2. Baseball
players.] I. Title. II. Series.
GV865.M396T56 1999
796.357'092—dc21
   [B]   98-33313
                                             CIP
                                             AC

To Our Readers:
All Internet addresses in this book were active and appropriate when we went to
press. Any comments or suggestions can be sent by e-mail to Comments@enslow.com
or to the address on the back cover.

Illustration Credits: AP/Wide World Photos, pp. 10, 12, 88; Carrol
Henderson, p. 83; Tacoma Raniers Baseball Club, p. 43; Stew Thornley,
p. 64; University of Southern California Athletic Department, pp. 23, 27;
Ron Vesely, pp. 17, 32, 40, 44, 52, 54, 59, 78, 80, 90.

Cover Illustration: AP/Wide World Photos.

Contents

Chapter 1

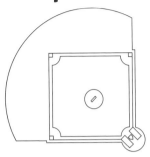

Number 62

The crowd stood and roared as Mark McGwire walked from the on-deck circle to the batter's box. It was his second trip to the plate in this game between his team, the St. Louis Cardinals, and the Chicago Cubs, on Tuesday night, September 8, 1998. The Cardinals were behind in the game, 2–0, and a home run from McGwire would help them catch up.

But the St. Louis fans had a different reason for wanting a home run. McGwire had already hit 61 home runs in the season. His next one would set a new major-league record for home runs in a single season. Roger Maris of the New York Yankees had set the record when he hit 61 homers in 1961. His record had held up for more than thirty-five years despite the attempts of many great sluggers to break it.

Finally, it looked as if the record was on the verge of being broken. Maris died in 1985, the year before Mark McGwire broke into the major leagues. Now, on this night, Maris's children were among the fans watching at Busch Stadium in St. Louis. They had some sad feelings that their dad's record wasn't going to last much longer. But they were also happy for McGwire.

The Maris family went through a tough time when Roger Maris was setting the record in 1961. Few people wanted Maris to break Babe Ruth's record of 60 home runs in one season, and even some of the fans of his own team, the New York Yankees, were against Maris. Not only that, but Maris was also competing with Mickey Mantle, a popular Yankee in 1961. Roger Maris's family remembered the way he was treated during the 1961 season. McGwire was more warmly received than Maris had been.

Another fan of McGwire's was Sammy Sosa, the right fielder for the Cubs. Sosa had 58 home runs and had been making a push for the record, too. For a while, it looked as if Sosa might break Maris's record before McGwire did. Even though they were competing against each other, as were their teams, Sosa and McGwire had been pulling for each other.

The night before, when McGwire had hit his 61st home run to tie the record, Sosa applauded.

McGwire had grounded out in his first time at bat in this game. On every pitch to him, fans throughout the stadium snapped photos, hoping to capture the historic home run on film. Thousands of flashes went off, making it look almost as if there were a lightning storm. On the first pitch of McGwire's second at bat, in the fourth inning, the lightning storm came again. Some of the light came from the flashbulbs, but one of the lightning bolts came from McGwire.

Chicago pitcher Steve Trachsel had delivered a low fastball. McGwire turned on the pitch and made solid contact. The ball shot off his bat and headed toward left field. He had hit it hard, but he wasn't sure whether the line drive would be high enough to make it over the fence. As McGwire ran to first base, he saw the ball clear the fence for his 62nd home run of the season.

The crowd exploded, and so did McGwire. He leaped into the air as he neared first base, and he embraced first-base coach Dave McKay. McGwire stopped to make sure he touched the bag before continuing his journey around the bases. Each of the Cubs infielders stuck out his hand to congratulate him. When McGwire reached home plate, he

Mark McGwire hit his record-breaking 62nd home run of the 1998 season in front of his home crowd. The game was delayed several minutes as fans at Busch Memorial Stadium celebrated his breaking Roger Maris's season home run record.

slapped hands with his teammates who had come out of the dugout to greet him. McGwire then lifted the team's ballboy off the ground and gave him a big hug. That ballboy was his son, Matt.

Matt lives in southern California with his mother and stepfather, but he often comes to St. Louis to watch his father play. When he does, he gets to wear a Cardinals uniform and serve as the team's ballboy. McGwire was happy that his son had a chance to be there for the historic moment. McGwire's parents were also there, in the stands with the other fans.

McGwire waved to the fans as his teammates continued to slap him on the back and congratulate him. Then one of the opposing players made it through the mob. It was Sammy Sosa, who had run in from right field. McGwire and Sosa hugged each other and celebrated.

McGwire had hugs for others. He stepped into the stands and went to see the Maris family, wrapping his arms around them. It was an emotional moment for Mark McGwire as well as for baseball fans everywhere.

In other stadiums around the league, the replay of McGwire's home run was shown on the jumbo screens on the scoreboards. Fans and players stood and cheered as their games were stopped.

The cheering in St. Louis lasted for more than ten

Mark McGwire celebrates his 62nd home run with first-base coach Dave McKay. McGwire was so excited that he almost missed touching first base.

minutes before the game resumed. McGwire's home run cut the Chicago lead, and the Cardinals later rallied for five more runs to win the game, 6–3.

McGwire's home run was hit down the left field line and barely cleared the fence, which is 330 feet from home plate. All season long, his home runs had been measured, with several estimated at more than 500 feet. McGwire was known not just for how often he hit home runs but also for how far he hit them. Even the pitchers he hit them off sometimes stood and watched in amazement. Orel Hershiser of the Cleveland Indians gave up a long blast to McGwire in 1996. "It's the longest home run I've ever given up," Hershiser said later. "It was awesome, one of those you admire."[1]

"Nobody misses a McGwire at bat," said Jason Giambi, McGwire's teammate that year, "because you never know how far the ball's going to go."[2]

However, fans didn't care that the record-breaking home run wasn't a tape-measure shot. Even though he had hit it hard, it was McGwire's shortest home run of the 1998 season. But it was one of the biggest home runs hit in the history of major-league baseball.

Chapter 2

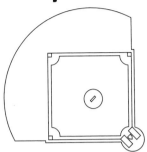

California Dreaming

Mark McGwire has dealt with a lot of injuries in his career, but he doesn't like to complain about them. He looks to his father, who put up with a lot more as he grew up.

John McGwire had polio, a disease that attacks the central nervous system and causes paralysis. At the age of seven, when he should have been outside playing with his friends, John was confined to his bed for several months. Even after he recovered, he walked with a limp and had to wear a leg brace.

But John wouldn't let it get in the way of his physical activities or keep him from enjoying life. He trained as an amateur boxer and learned to play golf. He strengthened his legs by riding his bicycle. Once he even rode more than three hundred miles, all the way from San Francisco to Santa Barbara, California.

John McGwire remained physically active when he grew up but had more on his mind than sports by this time. First, he studied to become a dentist. He also married and started a family in La Verne, California.[1] John and his wife, Ginger, had five children—all boys—Dan, Mark, Mike, Bob, and Jay, who was called J.J.

John McGwire had hoped his sons would want to be dentists, too. But all had other interests. J.J. hopes to be a bodybuilder, Bob became a contractor, and Mike became a psychologist. Dan, the tallest of the brothers at six feet eight inches, became a professional football player, playing quarterback for the Seattle Seahawks and Miami Dolphins.

As for Mark, he became a baseball player.

Mark McGwire was born on October 1, 1963, in Pomona, California. It soon became apparent to his family that baseball was his life. "As a boy, he'd lie on the floor watching baseball games on television," recalled his mother. "He wouldn't take the trash out as long as there was a game on. He always had that dream of playing in the major leagues."[2]

McGwire's parents served as role models to him. To this day, he believes that young people's heroes should be their parents, not movie stars, musicians,

FACT

McGwire's brother, Dan, played college football at both Iowa and San Diego State before entering the National Football League.

When Mark McGwire was growing up, he dreamed about playing major-league baseball. In 1986, his dream came true as he joined the Oakland Athletics late in the season.

or athletes.[3] From his dad, McGwire learned how hard work and determination could overcome difficulties in life.

When he was old enough, McGwire was eager to sign up and play Little League baseball. However, his parents weren't sure they wanted their son exposed to the pressure and high expectations associated with Little League. "I'd heard too much about arguing, meddling parents and bad coaches," McGwire's father said. "I didn't want anybody to screw up my son. When I told him he couldn't play, he cried and cried and cried."[4]

A year later, though, Mark's father found a Little League coach whom he liked in the nearby town of Claremont. This coach cared more about the young people he was coaching than about winning. Mark's father felt this coach treated his players well and didn't put too much pressure on them. Mark was finally allowed to play. He was eight years old and, in his first time at bat, faced a pitcher nearly four years older. Some thought the older pitcher would overpower the youngster. It was the other way around. McGwire connected and sent the ball sailing over the right-field fence for a home run.

"The surprising thing was he had an innate sense of how to play," said John McGwire of his son's experience in Little League. "He knew where to position players, he just knew. It was spine-tingling, his understanding of the game at such an early age. The old-timers who sat around the railroad tracks and talked baseball would say, 'This kid, he's something. He's going to light up the world.'"[5]

When he was ten, McGwire hit 13 home runs in one season. It was a Little League record in Claremont. But he could do more than just hit. McGwire was an ace pitcher with a blazing fastball.

Because of his skill on the baseball diamond—as well as his red hair, glasses, and height—McGwire stood out. Some young people like being noticed, but McGwire was just the opposite. "I was always the kind of kid who liked to sit in the back of the room and just blend in," McGwire said. "I was always just a basic athlete, nothing extraordinary. But I was a hard worker. And I like to do a lot of that work where people couldn't see me."[6] McGwire spent time hurling a ball off a cement wall and having it bounce back to him. McGwire would do this to practice his throwing by himself.

One of John McGwire's patients in the 1970s was Tommy John, a pitcher with the Los Angeles Dodgers. Tommy John and McGwire once played together in a celebrity golf tournament. "He used to tell me about how good his son was," Tommy recalled. "I thought he was just bragging."[7] A few years later Tommy John found out firsthand just how good Dr. McGwire's son was.

Mark McGwire didn't focus solely on baseball as a young boy. In fact, the first sport McGwire learned wasn't even baseball. It was golf. John McGwire had all his sons on the golf course when they were toddlers. McGwire learned from his father how to grip a club when he was five years old and never had another golf lesson of any kind. He picked up the sport naturally and won several tournaments as he got older. When he was in high school, McGwire even quit baseball for a year so he could concentrate on golf. "The thing I liked about golf was that you were the only one there to blame when something went wrong," he said. "I missed baseball, though, and I went back to it."[8]

As he grew up, McGwire played a variety of positions. He could handle playing third base or roaming the outfield in addition to being able to pitch.

He continued pitching and playing the field when he got to high school. At Damien High, an all-boys' private Catholic school in Claremont, McGwire played first base on the days he wasn't pitching. That way, the team could still keep his powerful bat in the lineup. One of the things that made McGwire successful on the diamond was his

FACT

An avid golfer, McGwire has played in the Pebble Beach ProAm with Billy Andrade, a professional golfer, as his partner.

attitude and even-tempered approach. "I've seen two or three other kids with the same kind of talent," his coach at Damien, Tom Carroll, said years later, "but it was Mark who went all the way."[9]

In his senior season, McGwire had a batting average of .359, highest on the Damien squad. He also had a 5–3 win-loss record as a pitcher with an earned-run average (ERA) of 1.90. An ERA indicates how many earned runs a pitcher allows, on the average, every nine innings. An ERA under 3.00 is very good. McGwire's ERA was more than one run better than that.

Even though there's no question he was a fine hitter, colleges and professional teams were looking at McGwire more as a pitcher. He was drafted by the Montreal Expos in June 1981. The Expos hoped to sign McGwire to a professional contract and have him pitch for one of their minor-league teams. If he did well, he would eventually reach the majors.

The Expos offered McGwire approximately fifteen thousand dollars to sign with them. But McGwire had other options. He might be able to receive a scholarship to go to college and play baseball. He would still have the opportunity to develop his baseball skills in addition to receiving an education.

Some top-notch high school players are recruited

FACT

While he was growing up, McGwire had an interest in law enforcement and thought about pursuing that as a career. He went on ride-alongs with police. One time he was along when the police raided a house on a drug arrest, and he watched as the police kicked in a door and entered the house with their guns drawn.

by a number of different colleges from across the country. That wasn't the case with McGwire, although a few college coaches did see him pitch in a high school tournament during McGwire's senior year at Damien and were impressed.

One of the coaches was an assistant for the Arizona State University Sun Devils. The Sun Devils flew him to their campus in Tempe, Arizona, and showed him around. They seemed interested in McGwire, but McGwire never heard from the school again.

However, soon after he got back from his trip to Arizona State, McGwire got a call from Rod Dedeaux, the head coach at the University of Southern California (USC) in Los Angeles. Art Mazmanian, a coach at a local two-year college and a former All-American baseball player for the USC Trojans, had also seen McGwire at the high school tournament. Mazmanian felt McGwire was too good to play at a two-year college, so he told Dedeaux about him.

Dedeaux and his pitching coach, Marcel Lachemann, arranged to come out and watch McGwire in action. McGwire did so well that he was offered a scholarship to USC.

He still had the chance to sign with the Montreal Expos organization. It would be exciting to be a professional baseball player. But McGwire knew the opportunity would still be there in a few years; if not with Montreal, then with another team.

He decided he was going to be a Trojan. He was going to go to college at the University of Southern California and play for the Trojans.

Rod Dedeaux coached the University of Southern California Trojans baseball team from 1942 to 1986. He was responsible for bringing Mark McGwire to the Trojans, as a pitcher, in 1981.

Chapter 3

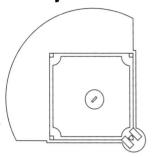

College Years

Right after McGwire accepted the scholarship offer from USC, he woke up with stomach pains and ended up in the hospital. He had appendicitis and had to have his appendix removed. If that wasn't bad enough, the doctor also discovered that McGwire had mononucleosis, whose symptoms are fever, chills, sore throat, and fatigue.

The only way to get over mononucleosis is to rest for many weeks. It meant that McGwire was done with baseball, and just about any other type of physical activity, for close to two months. In a way, though, the illness was a positive turning point for him.

After a layoff of almost eight weeks, McGwire began playing baseball for an American Legion

team in Claremont. As usual he pitched in some games and played the field in others. He didn't feel comfortable pitching and said he felt "as if I was starting over from scratch."[1] However, he did feel right at home at the plate. He had a batting average of .415 and hit 14 home runs that summer as he helped his team reach the state playoffs. McGwire said that summer of baseball caused him to begin thinking of himself more as a hitter than as a pitcher.[2]

However, Rod Dedeaux still had McGwire in mind as a pitcher for the University of Southern California. Dedeaux was a legend at USC. He had coached the Trojans for forty years, and the team had won 11 national championships during that time.

McGwire learned a great deal playing for Dedeaux, particularly about the mental aspects of the game. He began taking baseball seriously for the first time when he came to USC. McGwire quit relying just on his physical talent. Dedeaux made sure his players knew how to play baseball the right way, and he drilled his team on some of the fundamentals of the game. "Don't make the same mistake once," was one of Dedeaux's favorite sayings.[3] McGwire paid attention to that advice.

In 1982, McGwire's freshman season, he pitched in 20 games. Most of the time he was a relief pitcher, but he started 4 games. With a fastball that could reach nearly 90 miles per hour, McGwire put together a win-loss record of 4–4 with an ERA of 3.04. It wasn't a bad start to a college career, and he was definitely doing better as a pitcher than as a hitter. (He had a batting average of only .200 and hit just three home runs in 75 at bats in his freshman season.)

However, that summer he continued the process of moving away from pitching and becoming primarily a hitter. Players often work on their skills during the off-season in summer baseball leagues. He went to Alaska to play in a summer league with the Anchorage Glacier Pilots, expecting to pitch. Ron Vaughn, one of the assistant coaches at USC, was also an assistant with the Glacier Pilots. Vaughn decided that McGwire should play first base that summer so he could be in the everyday lineup. "I had seen him hit in high school and in practice," Vaughn said of McGwire. "I couldn't see wasting him on the mound."[4]

McGwire had an outstanding summer in Alaska. In 44 games with the Glacier Pilots, he had a batting average of .404. He also hit 10 home runs and had 44 runs batted in (RBIs).[5] Although he had come to Alaska to pitch, he took the mound only one time that summer.

McGwire made great progress as a player during his summer with the Glacier Pilots. He credits the

Mark McGwire began his college career as a pitcher for USC. He became such a good hitter that head coach Rod Dedeaux wanted him to play every game, so McGwire learned to play first base as well as pitch.

team's coach, Jim Dietz, for sticking with him and not benching him when he was in a slump. Spending a summer a long way from home also toughened McGwire mentally. "The environment in Alaska really helped me," he said.

> I was away from home for the first time in my life with a group of people I didn't know. I didn't have the support of my family and girlfriend, and I went through a very bad period of homesickness. But instead of quitting and going home, which would have been the easy thing to do, I stuck it out. As a result, I gained confidence in myself . . . and I grew up.[6]

When he got back to USC, McGwire told Dedeaux that he preferred playing first base to pitching. Dedeaux still wasn't convinced that changing McGwire from a pitcher to a full-time hitter was the thing to do. "When you take a guy who's an outstanding prospect as a pitcher and change him to another position, you've got to do a lot of thinking," Dedeaux said. "You don't want to burn any bridges."[7] What Dedeaux did in 1983 was give McGwire a chance to both pitch and play first base.

McGwire rewarded his coach by leading the team in home runs as a hitter and in earned-run average as a pitcher. On the mound, he started 7 games and had a win-loss record of 3–1 to go with his ERA of 2.78. (McGwire's ERA was more than twice as good as that of one of his teammates, a tall left-hander named Randy Johnson. Johnson, who had an ERA of 5.71 that season, would go on to become a star in the major leagues.)

However, it was McGwire's hitting that attracted more attention during his sophomore season. He hit 19 home runs, setting a new single-season record at USC. He broke the previous record of 17, which had been set by Kent Hadley in 1956 and tied by Dave Hostetler in 1978. Hadley and Hostetler both went on to play in the major leagues.

In addition to the home runs, McGwire produced a batting average of .319 and led the Trojans with 46 runs scored, 61 hits, and 59 RBIs in the 53 games in which he played. More important, he helped USC put together a record of 35 wins and 26 losses in 1983. During the 1970s, the Trojans had regularly won more than 50 games a season; however, in McGwire's freshman season, the team had won only 23 out of 59 games.

McGwire had another outstanding experience in the summer. He played first base for an American team that was sponsored by the United States Baseball Federation. The team competed in the Pan-American Games in Venezuela. McGwire hit

FACT

The USC Trojans played at Dedeaux Field when McGwire was in college. The stadium is located on the northwest corner of the USC campus and can hold nearly two thousand fans. The distances from home plate to the fences are 335 feet down the lines, 375 to the power alley in left center, 365 to right center, and 395 to straightaway center.

.454 with 6 home runs in 9 games. In addition to playing in the Pan-American Games, the American team played against different teams across the United States as well as around the world. McGwire ended up playing baseball in Japan, Belgium, and Holland in the summer of 1983. While he continued to improve as a hitter, McGwire spent a great deal of time working on his defense. He spent a lot of time fielding grounders and taking throws at first base to help him get better at that position.

When McGwire returned to USC at the end of the summer, Dedeaux was finally convinced that McGwire's future in baseball would be as a hitter rather than as a pitcher. "What sets McGwire apart from most college sluggers is his swing, remarkably effortless and compact," said Dedeaux. "He has the God-given gift of being able to drive the ball a long way without overswinging."[8]

Some power hitters take huge swings at pitches. They can hit some long home runs when they connect, but they also strike out a lot. The longer, harder swings that these players take make it more difficult to connect on pitches. McGwire had a compact swing. He struck out fewer times than a lot of other sluggers, and he could also hit the ball a long distance. He continued to refine his swing over the years, becoming even more efficient.

For his junior season at USC, McGwire set a goal of hitting 30 home runs. It was a high goal, but at least he would be concentrating only on hitting this year. He didn't get into a single game as a pitcher during the 1984 season.

The Trojans got off to a good start, winning 19 of their first 25 games. "This year we're hungry," McGwire said. "Everyone's disappointed when we lose. That's something I haven't seen here in the last two years."[9]

Three times during the year, McGwire was named the Pacific 10 Conference Player of the Week. Midway through the season, he hit the 40th home run of his career, breaking the conference record of 39 that had been set by Stan Holmes of Arizona State University.

McGwire ended up surpassing the goal he had set at the beginning of the season. He hit 32 home runs, setting a new conference single-season record, and he also had 80 RBIs and a batting average of .387 for the season.

Thanks in large part to McGwire, the Trojans made the National Collegiate Athletic Association playoffs for the first time since 1978.

Even though McGwire was only a junior and had a year of college eligibility left, he was expected to be one of the first players selected in the amateur

When he was in college, Mark McGwire worked on his hitting. At USC, McGwire developed the compact, powerful swing that would help him become a major-league player.

draft in June. Any team drafting McGwire would be taking a chance. After all, he might decide not to sign a professional contract, but continue in college, as he had done after the Montreal Expos had drafted him following his senior season in high school. The Oakland Athletics thought McGwire was worth that chance, though. They had the tenth overall pick in the draft and selected McGwire.

McGwire would have a choice to make—continue at USC or turn professional. However, he wouldn't have to make that choice right away. For now, he had other things to occupy his time.

Chapter 4

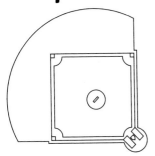

New Challenges

In 1984, baseball was a demonstration sport in the Olympic Games. At various times during the twentieth century, exhibition baseball games were played during the Olympics, but in 1984 a baseball tournament would be a part of the Olympics. It wasn't an official Olympic sport—that wouldn't happen until the 1992 Games—but it was still exciting to have exhibition baseball included in the Olympics.

It also afforded the opportunity to put together the best amateur players in the United States. McGwire was clearly one of the country's best amateur players in 1984, and he made the Olympic team, which was coached by Rod Dedeaux.

The selection process actually began in the fall of 1983 when 76 players assembled in Louisville,

Kentucky, for the pre-Olympic camp. These players had been invited by the United States Baseball Federation on the recommendation of college coaches. Dedeaux and his assistant coaches evaluated the players and invited forty players back to Louisville the following June. Eventually, the Olympic roster was trimmed to just twenty players, and McGwire was one of them.

The 1984 Olympics, which were held in Los Angeles, began in late July. Before this, though, the Olympic squad played games against a variety of professional and amateur opponents across the United States. It was a grueling schedule that called for the team to play games in thirty-three cities over a five-week span. "I call it the up-and-at-'em league," said Dedeaux. "We're up at 5 and at 'em all day. I've taught them to sleep fast. They stretch out in locker rooms, buses, airports. We're teaching them to get eight hours sleep in four."[1]

This schedule helped the players prepare for the busy life they would find once they went into professional baseball. Actually, it was a tougher grind than any of them expected ever to face again. McGwire went to cities he had never been to before but had little chance to see them. "I was in New York for the first time in my life, and all I saw was Shea Stadium and the inside of my hotel room."[2]

Shea Stadium is the home of the New York Mets. The Olympic team played many of its games in major-league stadiums, usually before a major-league game. Often, the major-league players would get to the stadium early enough to watch the Olympic players. The major-leaguers wanted to see whom they would be playing with, or against, in the near future. That was the case at Fenway Park in Boston in early July. Reggie Jackson was one of the major-league players watching when McGwire unloaded a long home run to center field.

Jackson was a great slugger himself and would often stand at home plate and admire a long shot he had hit before running the bases. After the game, he tried to convince McGwire that he should do the same. "Son, when you hit a ball like that, you've got to watch it," Jackson said. "No, that's not my style," replied McGwire.[3] The low-key approach to hitting home runs fit with McGwire's overall personality.

Three days after the blast at Fenway Park, McGwire and the rest of the Olympic team were across the country in San Francisco, playing in Candlestick Park, home of the Giants. This time, the spectators included members of the major-league All-Star teams, who would be playing the following evening. In its game, the Olympic team beat a team from Japan, 8–0, as McGwire drove in 2 runs.

McGwire played in 30 games during the pre-Olympic tour and hit .391 while driving in 26 runs. Eight countries participated in the Olympic baseball tournament; in addition to the United States, there was Canada, Korea, Taiwan, Japan, the Dominican Republic, Nicaragua, and Italy.

The United States won its first three games—beating Taiwan, Italy, and the Dominican Republic—to advance to the semifinal round. The United States came away with a 5–2 win over Korea and now would play for the gold medal. More than fifty-five thousand fans were on hand to see the final game, which the United States lost, 6–3, to Japan. McGwire and his teammates received Olympic silver medals. McGwire had not done as well in the Olympics as he had during the countrywide tour that preceded it. In the Olympics he had only 4 hits in 21 at bats for a .190 batting average. Still, it was an extremely valuable experience. He had the chance to play with some of the best amateur players in the country, players he would later play with and against in the majors.

With the Olympics over, it was time to move on. McGwire decided to forgo his senior season at USC and become a pro baseball player. He signed a contract with the Oakland Athletics and was immediately assigned to their minor-league team in

FACT

McGwire received the President's Award as the Most Valuable Player (MVP) on the USA baseball team in 1984. He was named co-MVP of the Pacific 10 Conference Southern Division, along with Arizona State's Oddibe McDowell. McGwire was also named a first-team All-American at first base.

Modesto, California. Modesto was a Class A team. (Major-league teams have farm systems, consisting of minor-league teams, to develop their young players. Class AAA is the highest level in the minors. Class A is two levels below that.)

By the time McGwire joined Modesto, there wasn't much left of the 1984 season. McGwire played in 16 games and had trouble adjusting to the new level of pitching that he was facing. He had only one home run and struck out 21 times. However, such a brief period is not long enough to judge a player. McGwire would be back with a chance at a full season.

During the off-season, Mark married his college sweetheart, Kathy. He had met Kathy while both attended USC. The couple married in December 1984. However, Mark could not always be there for Kathy, because his baseball career eventually forced him to travel across the continent for most of the year. The couple tried to make the marriage work while Mark was playing in the minors, but by the time McGwire made a name for himself in the major leagues, their relationship was crumbling.

He got off to a slow start in 1985 and was hitting only .217. "I struggled pretty much in the beginning of the year," McGwire said. "Then I began to realize there's always another day."[4]

The Oakland Athletics chose McGwire with the tenth overall choice in the 1984 draft. It would not take long for McGwire to move up through the A's farm teams to the major leagues.

By the end of June, McGwire was in a groove. In a game against the San Jose Bees on June 30, McGwire broke up a no-hit bid by George Ferran of San Jose in the sixth inning. It led to Modesto's first run of the game and helped the team to a 2–0 win. In addition, it extended McGwire's hitting streak to 21 games (meaning that he had had at least one hit in each game for 21 games in a row).

By the time of the California League All-Star Game in mid-July, McGwire was hitting .314, with 17 home runs and 75 runs batted in. McGwire was one of four Modesto infielders in the starting lineup for the Northern Division in the All-Star Game.

McGwire was playing infield for Modesto in 1985 but at a different position—third base instead of first base. He had some problems at his new position, committing 23 errors at third base, the second-highest total in the league. But at least his hitting was back on track. For the season, McGwire had a batting average of .274, as well as tying for the California League lead in home runs, with 24, and RBIs, with 106. He was also named the California League Rookie of the Year.

His performance earned him a promotion to Huntsville, the Athletics' Class AA farm team, in 1986. He wasn't there long, though. After hitting 10 home runs and driving in 53 runs in only 55 games,

FACT

McGwire played minor-league baseball in Modesto in 1984 and 1985 and remembered the community when it was ravaged by a flood years later. In 1997, McGwire and two of his former teammates on the Oakland Athletics donated $20,000 to start a fund drive to help flood victims in Modesto.

McGwire was moved up again. On June 6 he was assigned to the Athletics' Class AAA team in Tacoma, just a step away from the major leagues. Once again, his stay was brief. He continued to hit well and, as a result, was called up to the majors by the Athletics on Wednesday, August 20, 1986.

McGwire joined the Athletics in Baltimore, but in his first days as a major-leaguer, he saw nothing but rain. Oakland's games against the Orioles were rained out on both Wednesday and Thursday. The team moved on to New York for a weekend series. This time the weather was better. The Athletics were able to play their games against the Yankees, and McGwire was in the starting lineup, playing third base, in all of them.

In his first game, on Friday, August 22, McGwire was hitless in three at bats. He was 0–for–3 again on Saturday. However, on Sunday, August 24, he broke loose.

McGwire came up against Tommy John, a crafty left-hander and Dr. McGwire's former patient. Mark McGwire was up in the second inning, and he stroked a single to center off John for his first hit in the majors. After grounding out in his next at bat, McGwire came to the plate in a key situation in the sixth inning. The Yankees were ahead by one run, but Oakland had a runner on second base. McGwire

McGwire only played for two years in the minor leagues before he became a major-leaguer. He had a brief stop in Tacoma, Washington, playing for the Tigers (now known as the Raniers), before being promoted to the Oakland A's.

Mark McGwire needed some time to adjust to major-league pitchers before he became the great hitter he is today. In his first year of major-league baseball, he batted only .189 in 18 games. The next season, he batted .289 over 151 games.

doubled to drive in the tying run. He later scored in the inning, to put the Athletics ahead.

Oakland couldn't hold the lead, though. The Yankees were ahead, 4–3, when McGwire came to the plate in the eighth inning. Tommy John was no longer pitching for New York. McGwire singled to left against relief pitcher Rod Scurry. It was the start of a big inning for the Athletics. McGwire came around to score the tying run. He was followed by three teammates. McGwire's third hit of the game had sparked a four-run rally that propelled the Athletics to victory.

McGwire got another thrill in his next game when he hit his first major-league home run. It came at Tiger Stadium in Detroit and was a long drive to center field.

McGwire stayed the rest of the season with Oakland. He hit only .189 in 18 games, but the Athletics planned to have him back with them for an entire season in 1987. Also, the team was wondering whether it should keep McGwire at third base. McGwire made a lot of errors at that position, and the Athletics thought about moving him back to first base or even trying him in the outfield.

Although there was some uncertainty about his fielding and where he should play, there was little question that he was going to do well as a hitter.

Chapter 5

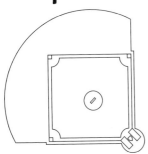

Rookie Wonder

Even though he had been with the Athletics in 1986, McGwire was still classified as a rookie (first-year player) in 1987. He did not have enough at bats in 1986 for it to be considered a full season. He didn't play in the opening game of the 1987 season. Rob Nelson, a left-handed hitter, played first base in that game. The Athletics planned on using both Nelson and McGwire as their first basemen. However, Nelson didn't hit well, and he was sent to the minors within two weeks. That left the team's full-time first-base position to McGwire—if he could handle it. He quickly proved that he could.

McGwire hit 4 home runs in April. That wasn't an impressive total, but as it turned out, he was just warming up. In early May, the Athletics played a three-game series against the Tigers in Detroit, the stadium where McGwire had hit his first homer in the majors the previous season. In the first game of the series, McGwire hit 2 home runs. The next day he homered again. In the final game of the series, the Athletics faced the Tigers' top pitcher, Jack Morris. That didn't stop McGwire. He homered twice off Morris, giving him 5 home runs for the series and 10 for the season, including one earlier in May.

McGwire was on a roll. He continued to hit home runs and had 19 by the end of May. That was an impressive number of home runs at such an early point in the season.

His final two home runs of the month were hit off an old friend, Tommy John. After that game, McGwire talked to his dad on the phone and told him what he had done to his father's former dental patient. "Tell Tommy he's overdue for a checkup," joked John McGwire. "I owe him a free cleaning—one for each home run."[1]

It was turning into a good season for young first basemen on both sides of the San Francisco Bay. Oakland is on the east side of the bay. San Francisco, home of the Giants, is on the west side. While McGwire was having a big year with the Athletics, Will Clark was doing a great job as the first baseman for the Giants. McGwire and Clark had been teammates on the 1984 Olympic team.

McGwire continued to hit home runs at a rapid pace in June, topping it off with a fabulous weekend performance in Cleveland against the Indians. On Saturday, June 27, McGwire hit 3 home runs, scored 5 runs, and drove in 5 runs. The next day, he hit 2 more home runs and scored 4 more. In just two games, McGwire had 8 hits, 7 RBIs, 9 runs scored, and 5 home runs.

At this point, McGwire had 27 home runs for the season and was on his way to setting a new single-season home run record for rookies. The rookie record was 38, set by Wally Berger of the Boston (now Atlanta) Braves in 1930 and matched by Frank Robinson of the Cincinnati Reds in 1956. There seemed no doubt McGwire would pass that mark.

He was also on pace for an even greater record—the single-season home run record of 61, set by Roger Maris of the New York Yankees in 1961.

Because of this, McGwire began receiving a great deal of attention, especially from sports reporters, and it didn't make it any easier for him to do his job. After McGwire's big series in Cleveland in June, the Athletics went to Chicago to play the White Sox. When McGwire got to his locker before the game, he found twenty-five reporters waiting to talk to him.

Reporters became a familiar sight to McGwire for the rest of the season. "For three months, there wasn't a time when I came to a park that there wasn't somebody waiting for me at my locker," McGwire said later.

> I like to get to the park early and kick back for a while before I start thinking about the game. But I had no chance to do that. It affected my concentration, because I couldn't get in the right frame of mind. I had never thought much about records, but there was always somebody there to remind me of them.[2]

McGwire had a teammate in 1987 who knew what he was going through. Reggie Jackson was playing the final season of his great career. Back in 1969, playing for Oakland in only his second full season in the majors, Jackson had gotten off to a great start. He had hit 34 home runs by early July and experienced the same crush of attention from reporters and fans that McGwire was experiencing. Jackson tailed off over the last half of the season but still finished the year with 47 home runs.

Jackson was able to provide a good influence for McGwire as well as for Jose Canseco, another young slugger on the team. Canseco and McGwire had played together in the minors, but Canseco had arrived in the major leagues first. He had been the

American League's Rookie of the Year in 1986 and was one of the top hitters in baseball in 1987. Canseco and McGwire provided a great power punch in the Oakland lineup. The two became known as the "Bash Brothers."

Another calming influence on McGwire was the manager of the Athletics, Tony LaRussa. LaRussa is considered one of the top managers in baseball, and McGwire has great respect for him. McGwire felt comfortable in Oakland because he liked playing for LaRussa.

The 1987 All-Star Game was played at Oakland-Alameda County Coliseum, the home of the A's. McGwire had 33 home runs by the All-Star break and was a member of the American League All-Star team. He played in the game, although he did not get any hits.

When the season resumed after the All-Star break, McGwire continued his assault on the record books. Meanwhile, the Athletics pursued the Minnesota Twins for first place in the American League Western Division. McGwire finished July with 37 home runs, and the A's were in second place, staying close to the top spot.

On Tuesday, August 11, in Seattle, McGwire hit his 38th home run of the season, tying the rookie record. Three days later, in Anaheim, he broke a 3–3

McGwire had a great rookie season in 1987. He hit 49 home runs and was named to the American League All-Star Team. The All-Star Game was played at Oakland-Alameda County Coliseum, the home of the Oakland A's.

tie in the sixth inning with a two-run homer off Don Sutton (who is now a member of the Baseball Hall of Fame). McGwire now held the single-season home run record for rookies.

The name McGwire was becoming well known in the sports world. As Mark McGwire was slugging home runs, his younger brother, Dan, was starting his college football career with the University of Iowa. But it was clear which McGwire was on the mind of fans and announcers. As Dan made his first start at quarterback, the public-address announcer introduced him by saying, "At quarterback for Iowa, Mark . . . Dan McGwire."[3]

After breaking the rookie record, McGwire cooled off a bit, hitting only one more home run in August. His slump destroyed any hopes of breaking Roger Maris's record; however, he still had a good chance of reaching 50, a great total in any season. To that point, only ten other players had ever hit that many homers in a season. For McGwire to reach that level in his first full year in the major leagues would be an amazing achievement.

McGwire got back in the groove in September. Unfortunately, the A's tailed off and dropped out of contention in the pennant race. The only exciting question left in the final week of the season was whether McGwire could reach 50 home runs. He hit

FACT

In 1987 McGwire came close to being only the eleventh player ever to hit 50 or more home runs in a season in the major leagues. The others were Babe Ruth, Roger Maris, Jimmie Foxx, Hank Greenberg, Hack Wilson, Ralph Kiner, Mickey Mantle, George Foster, Willie Mays, and Johnny Mize. Ruth did it four times. Foxx, Kiner, Mantle, and Mays each did it twice.

After a fantastic 1987 season, Mark McGwire ran away with the American League Rookie of the Year award. Every vote cast for Rookie of the Year was for McGwire.

his 49th on Tuesday, September 29, but he didn't connect in the next four games. The Athletics had one game left, on Sunday, October 4, in Chicago. It would be McGwire's last shot at the milestone.

However, something more important to him was happening. Back in California, his wife, Kathy, was expecting their first child. McGwire skipped the team's final game to be with her as she gave birth to their son, Matthew. McGwire never regretted missing that last game. "You'll always have a chance to hit 50 home runs. You'll never have a chance to have your first child again." Referring to his newborn son, McGwire said, "That was my 50th home run."[4]

Chapter 6

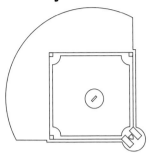

World Champs

Mark McGwire was named the American League's Rookie of the Year in 1987. He was only the second player to be a unanimous choice for Rookie of the Year in the American League. (Carlton Fisk of the Boston Red Sox was the other, in 1972.)

In addition to his 49 home runs, most in the American League, McGwire had driven in 118 runs and had a batting average of .289 in 1987.

It would be a hard act to follow. McGwire still had an outstanding season in 1988, although not quite as good as his rookie year. But he didn't generate nearly as much attention. One reason was that there was more focus on team performance. The A's won their first division title since 1981 and advanced to the playoffs.

Another reason was that McGwire's teammate, Jose Canseco, was grabbing the headlines. Canseco became the first player in history to have at least 40 stolen bases and 40 home runs in the same season. Canseco finished the regular season with 42 home runs, tops on the team.

McGwire played a role in his teammate's success. He normally batted right after Canseco, which helped Canseco get better pitches to hit. Power hitters often get pitched around, which means that pitchers don't want to serve up anything too easy to hit. Pitchers would rather miss the strike zone and end up walking the hitter than risk putting one over the heart of the plate. It can be very frustrating for good hitters to have this happen, and it's more likely to happen if there is not another good hitter following them in the order.

However, when a batter is backed up with another slugger, it helps him to see good pitches to hit. This was the case with Canseco and McGwire. Pitchers knew if they walked Canseco, that would be just one more runner aboard for a batter like McGwire to drive in.

American League pitchers had a lot to fear when they got to the heart of the Oakland batting order. "You have to be extremely careful when you face them," said Chris Bosio of the Milwaukee Brewers,

The 1989 Oakland Athletics had a power-packed lineup. Other teams not only had to face McGwire, but also Jose Canseco (left) and Terry Steinbach (middle), who provided extra power to the A's offense. Canseco and McGwire would become known as the "Bash Brothers."

a team that was in the American League at that time. "Because at any given time, they can take your head off with one swing of the bat. It's like facing two clones—two big, six-foot five-inch, 240-pound muscleheads."[1]

Reggie Jackson had retired and was no longer with the Athletics, but both Canseco and McGwire had learned about the impact of home runs from their 1987 teammate. "People remember the damage," Jackson had told the pair.[2]

Even though they could both do a lot of damage, there were differences in how the Bash Brothers went about doing it. "We're two different hitters," said McGwire. "I like to swing nice and fluid and easy. Jose swings hard. When I swing hard, I get myself in trouble."[3]

"The most noticeable thing about him is that he is a big man with a compact swing," said the Athletics' hitting coach, Bob Watson, about McGwire. McGwire uses more than just his arms to generate his power. He crouches at the plate, to use the strength in his legs when he uncoils and swings.

McGwire finished the 1988 regular season with 32 home runs—a good total, although considerably lower than his record in 1987. He also had 99 runs batted in and would have topped 100 again if not for back stiffness that caused him to miss nine of

Oakland's last sixteen games of the regular season. Back problems would continue to plague him throughout his career.

McGwire was feeling better as the A's faced the Boston Red Sox, champions of the Eastern Division, in the American League Championship Series. The winner of this series would advance to the World Series. Oakland beat the Red Sox easily, with McGwire hitting .333 with one home run during the series.

The Athletics were heavy favorites in the 1988 World Series against the Los Angeles Dodgers. Jose Canseco hit a grand slam in the first game, and the A's had a 4–3 lead with two out in the last of the ninth. But then Oakland reliever Dennis Eckersley walked Mike Davis of the Dodgers and gave up a two-run homer to Kirk Gibson that won the game for the Dodgers. Los Angeles won the next game to go up by two games in the best-of-seven series.

Oakland knew it had to win the next game to have a realistic chance of coming back in the series. The third game was tied, 1–1, in the last of the ninth when McGwire stepped into the batter's box to face Dodgers relief ace Jay Howell. McGwire connected with one of Howell's pitches and sent a long drive to left field. It was obvious as soon as it left his bat that it would be a home run. The blast gave the Athletics a 2–1 win and pulled them to within one game of the Dodgers.

However, that was as close as they would come. The Dodgers won the next two games to finish off the Athletics and win the World Series, 4 games to one. McGwire's game-winning home run in the third game was his only hit of the series.

It had been a great year for Oakland, but it had a disappointing finish. For McGwire, there was other pain to deal with. He and Kathy were having marital problems. They tried hard to work things out but finally decided to get a divorce. The two split on friendly terms. "Kathy and I are very good friends, and we have a beautiful child," said McGwire. "We're going to see each other the rest of our lives because we have Matthew. I love my kid to death. We're going to make it a positive thing where he can grow up in two households."[4]

Sometimes personal problems will affect a player's performance, but McGwire maintained his composure on the field despite the difficulties he was going through off the field. His manager, Tony LaRussa, was impressed with how McGwire was able to deal with the situation and separate his personal life from his baseball career.

The Athletics were determined to get back to the World Series in 1989 and to win it.

Oakland had some injuries to contend with right from the beginning. Canseco missed the team's first eighty-eight games with a wrist injury. McGwire also sat out fourteen games in April with a herniated disk in his back.

Nonetheless, Oakland was a well-rounded team and played well even without its major stars. The Athletics led the American League Western Division through most of May and June and finally moved into first place for good on August 21. They finished the regular season with the best record in baseball for the second straight year.

After his early-season injury, McGwire came back to finish the year with 33 home runs, tops on the team and third in the American League. Oakland met Toronto in the league playoffs and had little trouble with the Blue Jays, beating them, 4 games to one. The Athletics were going back to the World Series.

McGwire said, regarding Oakland's return to the World Series:

> The 1988 series gave us something to keep in the back of our minds for 1989. We had a great team last year, but we didn't get the job done. Against the Dodgers, we forgot some of the little things that made it possible to get to the series. We all tried to hit the ball out of the park against the Dodgers. And we lost. Now we're

FACT

Mark McGwire studies videotapes of opposing pitchers. He says it helps him build a mental file on each pitcher he faces. "It gives me a better chance every time I get in the box."[5]

back in the Series. And this time around, we won't forget the little things. We're stronger than we were in 1988. We've got some new parts for our engine. We have a more complete team than we did a year ago.[6]

One of the new parts was Rickey Henderson, a former star for the A's who had been with the Yankees the previous few years. Henderson came back to Oakland in a trade in June and provided the team with a great spark. He led the majors with 77 stolen bases, with 52 of them coming after the trade. In the five-game playoff series versus Toronto, Henderson stole 8 bases and scored 8 runs. Henderson was a great addition to the team, with his ability to get on base with sluggers like McGwire and Canseco coming up.

Rickey Henderson, one of McGwire's teammates in Oakland, provided the 1989 A's with speed. Henderson would steal bases, while McGwire and Jose Canseco would drive in the runs.

Oakland's opponent in the World Series was the San Francisco Giants, the team from across the bay. The teams wouldn't have to travel far to get between the two stadiums.

The series opened in Oakland, and the Athletics won both games played there. Then they moved to Candlestick Park in San Francisco. The third game was scheduled for Tuesday, October 17. The starting lineups were about to be introduced when the players and fans in the stadium felt a rumbling. It was an earthquake. The San Francisco-Oakland area is located along the San Andreas Fault, and as a result, the region is prone to earthquakes. Some are mild, but this one wasn't. It was a massive quake that caused serious damage in the Bay Area and the loss of dozens of lives.

Players and fans remained calm in Candlestick Park. It was apparent the game would not be played that night. In fact, it was another ten days before the World Series resumed. The A's picked right up from where they had started before the long delay. They won the next two games, to win the World Series. McGwire didn't homer in the series, but he did have 5 hits in 17 at bats for an average of .294. Most important to him, however, was the fact that his team won. The Oakland Athletics were world champions.

The 1990 season was another good one for McGwire and the Athletics. For the third straight season, McGwire was voted by the fans to be the starting first baseman in the All-Star Game, played at Wrigley Field in Chicago in July. The following month, McGwire hit a grand slam in the 10th inning to give the Athletics a 6–2 win over Boston. It was his 30th home run of the year, and it made McGwire the first player ever to hit at least 30 home runs in each of his first four full seasons.

McGwire finished the regular season with 39 home runs. He also had 108 runs batted in and led the major leagues by walking 110 times. Oakland, after winning the division and sweeping Boston in the league playoffs, made it back to the World Series for the third year in a row. The Athletics, however, failed to win a game in the series, as they were swept by the Cincinnati Reds.

McGwire achieved a new honor in 1990. He received a Gold Glove, recognizing him as the best fielding first baseman in the league. Things were looking up in many ways for McGwire. However, he was struggling in one category—batting average. After he hit .289 in his rookie season, his batting average dropped over the next two seasons. He improved it slightly in 1990, but it was still only .235.

It would get worse before it got better.

Chapter 7

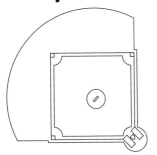

Downs and Ups

Mark McGwire's batting average went down again in 1991, this time dropping all the way to .201. He hit only 22 home runs. That's a pretty good total for most players, but not for McGwire. It was the first full season in which he didn't hit at least 30 home runs. If all this wasn't bad enough, the Athletics failed to win their division title for the first time since 1987.

When the season ended, McGwire got into his car and drove from Oakland to southern California, where he lived in the off-season. He didn't turn on the radio. He just wanted to think. He thought about how, for the first time, he disliked baseball. He also thought about how important the mental aspect of baseball is. "It took the failure of '91 to realize this game is mental," he said later. "You can play on ability for only so long."[1]

McGwire decided he should get some help with dealing with the mental part of the game. He began seeing a psychiatrist and, as he said, "getting my mind back together. . . . I started putting more effort into using my mind."[2]

During the winter between the 1991 and 1992 seasons, McGwire took up weight lifting. It helped him physically as well as mentally. "Weightlifting [sic] relieved a lot of the pain I was going through following the '91 season," he said. "When I started to see the changes in my body, it made me feel a lot more positive, more confident in myself."[3]

In addition to the weight lifting—which gave him added muscle as well as relief from stress— McGwire worked on his swing. A lot of power hitters have a big looping swing, which enables them to hit the ball with a lot of force. McGwire's swing always had been more compact, and now he refined it even more. Doug Rader, the Athletics' hitting coach, thought that the extra strength McGwire got from weight lifting helped with the swing. "The strength gives you confidence not to force the bat through the strike zone," Rader explained. "It eliminates the temptation to swing out of control. The less you have to do in a swing, the easier it is."[4]

All the work in the off-season paid off. McGwire was off to a great start in 1992. He had 10 home runs in April and then homered on each of the first three days in May—all at Tiger Stadium, a favorite launching pad for him. By mid-May McGwire was leading the major leagues with 15 home runs and 30 runs batted in.

He continued to lead the league in homers until he strained a rib muscle on August 21. He was placed on the disabled list and missed the next twenty games. By the time he came back, he was no longer in the lead. Juan Gonzalez of the Texas Rangers had passed him. McGwire finished the regular season with 42 home runs. It was one behind Gonzalez, who took the league home run crown, but it was a great improvement over his dismal 1991 season. McGwire also raised his batting average to .268. He was named the Comeback Player of the Year in 1992 by United Press International.

The Athletics also came back that year. Oakland won the Western Division title for the fourth time in five years; however, the Athletics were beaten by the Toronto Blue Jays in the league playoffs and didn't make it back to the World Series.

McGwire was a free agent after the 1992 season, and he was free to sign with any team in the major leagues. He decided to stay with the Oakland

Athletics, and he signed a new contract with the team in late December. He wanted to help the Athletics make it into the playoffs again.

That didn't happen. The 1992 season was the last year that Oakland won its division title. There would also be some personal frustration for McGwire over the next few years. He would play well—when he was in the lineup. The problem was that he often wasn't. McGwire had a lot of injuries, which cut down on his playing time tremendously.

McGwire was off to a strong start in 1993, but he injured his left heel during a series in New York in early May. He played in nine more games but finally had to come out of the lineup. He was placed on the disabled list and didn't come back until September. He pinch hit a couple of times, but it was obvious that the foot still wasn't healed. He had surgery on the heel and hoped that would be the end of his injury problems.

It wasn't. In April 1994, he suffered a stress fracture in his left heel and went back on the disabled list. He was out for more than six weeks. Then, in late July, he hurt the heel again and went back on the disabled list. He eventually underwent surgery on the heel again and missed the rest of the season.

McGwire played in only 74 games over the 1993 and 1994 seasons. The injury problems continued in

1995, although he played more, appearing in 104 games. During that season, McGwire was able to hit 39 home runs and drive in 90 runs.

Injuries had caused McGwire to miss 290 games over the last three seasons. However, he felt good when he came to spring training in 1996 and hoped that he could play a full season without having to miss time because of injuries. Unfortunately, that wasn't the case.

The left foot—the one that had given him problems the last three years—appeared to finally be fully healed. However, he ended up having the same troubles with his right foot. In a spring-training game in mid-March, McGwire raced all the way around the bases, scoring from first on a double by teammate Terry Steinbach. In doing so, McGwire broke the plantar fascia, a sheath of tissue that supports the arch, in his right foot. This was the same thing that had happened with his left foot.

The start-and-stop running that baseball players do puts pressure on the bottoms of their feet. For some players, this is no problem; for other players, it is. McGwire was one of those other players. As a result of the injury to the right foot, McGwire would have to miss the start of the 1996 regular season. At that point, he wondered whether he wanted to come back at all. He felt so frustrated that he thought

FACT

By 1996, two more players had reached 50 home runs since Mark McGwire's rookie season. Cecil Fielder of the Detroit Tigers hit 51 home runs in 1990. Albert Belle of the Cleveland Indians hit 50 home runs in 1995. In 1996 both McGwire and Brady Anderson of the Baltimore Orioles joined the 50-homer club.

about retiring from baseball. However, his friends and family urged him to keep going. He did.

McGwire missed the first eighteen games of the regular season and needed a little time to get going after that. In mid-May, though, he hit his stride. He was on a tear, hitting 21 home runs in 36 games between May 17 and June 27. He was named the Player of the Month in the American League in June.

One thing that helped McGwire in 1996 was a change that had been made to the Oakland-Alameda County Coliseum, the stadium in which the Athletics played their home games. A large seating area had been added in center field. The additional seats were wanted by the Oakland Raiders football team, which shared the stadium with the Athletics. However, the seats also affected baseball. They cut down on the winds that blew in from center field toward home plate. Before this happened, the Oakland-Alameda County Coliseum was considered a difficult place to hit home runs because of those winds. But the new seats, by blocking some of the wind, made the stadium an easier place to hit home runs.

On September 14, McGwire hit his 50th homer of the season. He got the milestone ball back and gave it to his son, Matt. Nine years before, McGwire had passed up his final chance to hit his 50th homer of the season so he could be present the day when Matt was born.

Tony LaRussa was no longer McGwire's manager in 1996. LaRussa by this time was managing the St. Louis Cardinals in the National League, and Art Howe was managing the Athletics. But LaRussa still admired McGwire, not just for his playing ability but for his determination in coming back from injuries. "He has not let frustration beat him," said LaRussa of McGwire.

> He has had some really tough recuperations and came back better each time. That meant he really had to do some disciplined work. When you do not play, you can get soft, and your skills erode. He is probably better, quicker, and stronger each time.[5]

McGwire finished the season with 52 home runs. He was the 13th player ever to reach 50 home runs. He was also the only player ever to hit at least 50 home runs while playing in fewer than 140 games in a season. In addition to the games he missed at the start of the season with the foot injury, McGwire sat out some other games in late July and early August with back problems. Had he been able to play the entire season, he might have had a chance that season at breaking Roger Maris's record of 61 home runs.

FACT

In 1996 McGwire became the first player to hit at least 50 home runs while playing in fewer than 140 games. He had one home run for every 8.13 at bats that season. Babe Ruth's best home run percentage came in 1920, when he had one home run for every 8.48 at bats. Roger Maris had one home run for every 9.67 at bats in 1961, the year he hit 61 home runs.

In 1996, McGwire averaged one home run for every 8.13 at bats. At that pace, McGwire would have broken the record if he hadn't missed so many games because of injuries.

"If he had been healthy," said his manager, Art Howe, during the season, "I don't think we would be talking about if he'd break the record. We'd be talking about when he'll break the record."[6]

Like Howe, many fans wondered what would happen if McGwire could get in a full season without being injured.

Chapter 8

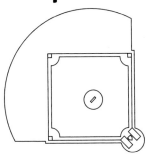

Chasing History

Mark McGwire was one person who refused to be caught up in the question of how many home runs he could have if not for the injuries.

> I've never been a guy that said, "What if?" You can't succeed as a player or a human being if you do that. You're not moving forward. You'd always be doubting yourself and wondering. I'm a pretty positive person. You've just got to deal with what's dealt to you.[1]

McGwire stayed healthy in 1997, and he ended up making a run at Maris's record. But he wasn't the only one. Sluggers like Ken Griffey, Jr., and Albert Belle had been producing big home run totals over the last few seasons.

McGwire had another good start in 1997. He had

11 home runs in April and hit another 8 in May. However, more attention was being focused on Griffey, a center fielder with the Seattle Mariners, who was hitting even more home runs.

By the end of May, Griffey had 24 home runs, the most ever hit by any player by that time of the season. McGwire, with 19 home runs, wasn't far behind. McGwire caught up with Griffey in June, and both players ended the month with 29 home runs. They were almost halfway to the record, with about half the season left.

However, both Griffey and McGwire went through a home run slump in July. Griffey hit only 3, and McGwire had 5. In July, McGwire had other things on his mind. He was in the last year of his contract with the Athletics and would be a free agent at the end of the season. This had happened after the 1992 season, and McGwire re-signed with Oakland. This time, though, the Athletics weren't sure that he would sign with them again. Many people thought McGwire might sign with one of the teams in southern California. His son, Matt, lived with his mother near Los Angeles. If McGwire played for a team like the Anaheim Angels or the Los Angeles Dodgers, he'd be able to see his son much more often during the season. Rather than risk losing McGwire to free agency and not getting anything in return for him, the Athletics thought about trading him.

Throughout July, there were rumors that McGwire would be traded. Finally, on the last day of the month, it happened. Oakland traded McGwire to the St. Louis Cardinals for three pitchers. The Cardinals, like the Athletics, weren't sure they'd be able to sign McGwire at the end of the season, but they decided to take a chance and trade for him anyway. They'd at least have him for the rest of the 1997 season, and McGwire might be able to help them make the playoffs.

McGwire would not only be changing teams, but also changing leagues. The Cardinals were in the National League. McGwire would have a different group of pitchers to hit against. He wouldn't be familiar with most of the pitchers and would have to learn about them.

At least one thing would be familiar—his manager. Tony LaRussa, who had managed the Athletics for many years, was now the manager in St. Louis. McGwire was happy about being reunited with LaRussa.

It took McGwire a little time to adjust to the new league and the different pitchers. He joined the Cardinals when the team was on a road trip, and he struggled at the plate. On Friday night, August 8, he

On July 31, 1997, Mark McGwire was traded from Oakland to the St. Louis Cardinals. He finished the year in St. Louis with 58 home runs for the season.

played his first game in Busch Stadium in St. Louis. The crowd gave McGwire a standing ovation his first time up. He popped out, but in his next at bat, he gave the fans what they wanted. He drilled a pitch down the left-field line and into the seats for his first National League home run.

McGwire was a big hit with the St. Louis fans. They showed up early to watch him take batting practice. Even opposing players stopped warming up and turned to watch when McGwire stepped into the batting cage. McGwire hit 9 home runs his first month with the Cardinals, giving him a total of 43 for the year.

Back in the American League, Ken Griffey was also doing well. He had 44 home runs by the end of August. Griffey and McGwire battled each other over the last month to see who would be the leading home run hitter in the major leagues. Griffey finished with 56, not a new record but a great total. McGwire did even better. In the next-to-last game of the season, McGwire hit 2 home runs to pass Griffey. He homered again the next day to finish his season with 58 home runs—34 with Oakland and 24 with St. Louis.

McGwire had thought that, when the season ended, he'd be deciding what team he would be playing for in 1998. However, when the time came,

No matter what happens, Mark McGwire always has time for the fans. Here he is signing autographs before a St. Louis Cardinals game.

he had already made his decision. On September 16, McGwire signed a contract extension with the Cardinals.

As soon as he signed the contract extension, McGwire announced that he was setting aside one million dollars a year to start a foundation to help abused children. A friend of McGwire's worked as a volunteer with children who had been sexually abused. She talked about the children she worked with to McGwire, who said, "Something has to be done."[2]

McGwire did something about it, not just with his money but also with his time. Over the off-season, he checked out facilities in St. Louis and southern California and decided where the money should go. He talked to abuse victims and listened to their stories. Susan Stepleton of the Edgewood Children's Center in St. Louis, which houses abused and neglected children, said McGwire's commitment to abused children was:

> wonderful news. A lot of sports heroes are willing to stand up for kids with heart or vision or breathing problems, but there's so much stigma around the issue of abuse and neglect. It's so painful, people shy away from it.[3]

Near the end of 1997, McGwire was named Sportsman of the Year by *The Sporting News*. The honor was not just for his great season but for the kind of person he is.

Away from baseball, McGwire likes to get away from the spotlight. He is an avid golfer and goes to a lot of movies. He also enjoys going to comedy clubs. "The wonderful thing about comedians is that they take some of our greatest fears and laugh them off. They make something funny out of some very serious stuff."[4] McGwire keeps that in mind whenever he is going through a slump in baseball.

The most important thing to McGwire is his son. "Everything I do in the game is for him. We have such a great relationship."[5]

Great things were expected of McGwire in 1998. This was the year, many fans felt, that the home run record would finally fall. Many thought McGwire would be the most likely player to break it, and their expectations increased when McGwire homered in each of the first four games of the season.

McGwire didn't hit any more home runs for more than a week. But then he broke loose again. In a game against the Arizona Diamondbacks, McGwire hit 3 home runs, bringing his season total to 7. He finished the month of April with 11 home runs and continued his home run hitting in May. On May 8, in a game at New York against the Mets,

FACT

Before the 1998 season, only two players before McGwire had ever hit as many as 60 home runs in a single season. Babe Ruth of the New York Yankees had hit 60 home runs in 1927. Roger Maris of the Yankees hit 61 in 1961.

When the Cardinals played games on the road, visiting fans would fill the stadiums for a chance to see Mark McGwire. Many fans would show up hours early just to see McGwire take batting practice.

McGwire hit his 13th homer of the year. It was also the 400th in his career.

At the end of May, McGwire had 27 home runs, the most in the major leagues. No player before had ever hit that many home runs through May. McGwire had some problems with his back in early June and missed a few games. On his return to the lineup, he homered in his first at bat. The back problems didn't flare up again, and he was able to keep playing.

Another problem he met was one he expected. Pitchers were afraid to give him anything too good to hit. Sometimes they would purposely walk him. McGwire was frequently walked intentionally during the season. Even when pitchers did pitch to him, they often did it in such a way that they made sure they didn't throw any easy pitches in the strike zone for him to hit. They missed the strike zone with a lot of pitches, rather than giving McGwire a pitch he could drive, and he ended up with a lot of walks.

Getting on base by a walk helps the team, and McGwire looked as if he might have a chance to break the record for walks in a season: 170, set by Babe Ruth of the New York Yankees in 1923. Ruth was probably the greatest slugger in the history of baseball and held the single-season home run record until Roger Maris broke it. But people wouldn't be going to the ballpark to make a big fuss over setting a record for the most walks. Fans everywhere, and especially those in St. Louis, were hoping McGwire could break the home run record.

McGwire wasn't the only one with a chance at Roger Maris's record, though. Once again, Ken Griffey of the Seattle Mariners was doing well. People expected McGwire and Griffey to be doing what they were doing. However, there were other contenders emerging. Greg Vaughn of the San Diego Padres and Sammy Sosa of the Chicago Cubs had joined the home run record chase, as well. Sosa had hit 20 home runs during the month of June, to find himself among the leaders. While Vaughn and Griffey slowed down a bit, Sosa stayed hot through the summer months and challenged McGwire for the home run lead.

McGwire went through his own period where he wasn't hitting a lot of home runs. He connected 8 times in July and then had only 2 home runs during the first eighteen days of August. His slump had allowed Sosa to catch up with him. Both players had 47 home runs as their teams—the Cubs and the Cardinals—played at Wrigley Field in Chicago on Wednesday, August 19.

In the fifth inning of the game, Sosa hit his 48th home run of the year. It was the first time all season he had led the major leagues in home runs. The lead didn't last long, though. McGwire homered in the eighth inning. The game went into extra innings, and McGwire hit another one in the 10th inning.

The next day, in the first game of a doubleheader in New York, McGwire hit his 50th of the season. He became the first player in the major leagues ever to have three seasons in a row with 50 or more home runs. His first time up in the second game of the doubleheader, McGwire homered again.

Hitting 4 home runs in two days was a sign that the dry spell was over. He was back on pace to break Roger Maris's record. Whether he could stay ahead of Sammy Sosa, though, was another matter.

On August 30, Sosa hit his 54th homer of the year, to tie McGwire for the lead. That night, McGwire hit number 55 to move back out in front. The next day, Sosa hit another one, to tie McGwire again.

Before the season started, reporters asked McGwire whether he'd be able to break Maris's record. All along, he said it was too early to be thinking about it. McGwire said it wasn't worth talking about unless a player had at least fifty home runs going into September.

Going into September of 1998, two players had 55 home runs. The record appeared sure to be broken. Which player would be the one to break it?

McGwire made his bid with a big performance in Florida against the Marlins on the first two nights of September. He had 2 home runs in each of two consecutive games, raising his total to 59.

The Cardinals then headed home for five games in St. Louis. The local fans hoped he would break the record in front of them rather than on the road. On Saturday, September 5, McGwire hit his 60th home run, joining Babe Ruth and Roger Maris as the only players ever to reach that level in the major leagues.

Two days later, Sammy Sosa and the Chicago Cubs came to St. Louis for a two-game series. Sosa had 58 homers by this time, two behind McGwire. The first game of the series was played in the afternoon on Labor Day before a sellout crowd and a national television audience. His first time up, McGwire hit a long drive down the left-field line. It was clearly long enough to be a home run; the question was whether it would stay fair. It did. It was McGwire's 61st home run, tying him with Maris, whose children were in the stands, watching. McGwire received a great ovation from the fans, but the real celebration would come when he hit the next one to break the record.

Home run number 62 came the next night. The game was broadcast on national television, and it

When Mark McGwire hit his 62nd home run of the 1998 season, one of the first people to congratulate him was Sammy Sosa. Sosa and McGwire had been competing for the home run lead, but Sosa was also rooting for McGwire to break Roger Maris's record.

drew the most viewers for a baseball game in many years. The event was one of the most memorable moments in the history of baseball. McGwire had broken the thirty-seven-year-old record set by Roger Maris in 1961.

But neither the season nor the home run race between McGwire and Sosa was over yet. Over the final weeks of the regular season, the two battled back and forth. Sosa caught up with McGwire, but McGwire hit his 63rd of the season to move back in front. Sosa countered with another home run to tie up the race again.

The sparring between the pair continued. McGwire hit 2 more, but Sosa came back with 2 home runs in one game to catch McGwire. Going into the final weekend of the season, both McGwire and Sosa had 65 home runs. Sosa's Cubs were playing the Astros at Houston while McGwire and the St. Louis Cardinals were at home against the Montreal Expos.

In Houston, Sosa hit a long home run to go one up on McGwire. Sosa was now the record holder for home runs in a season. But not for long. Less than an hour later, McGwire crushed one in St. Louis. Both players now had 66 home runs.

The next day, McGwire regained the record by hitting 2 more. Sosa would finish the season with

McGwire's gaze skyward became a familiar sight to fans as another home run sails out of the ballpark.

66 home runs. McGwire had one game to play, and fans wondered whether he could reach 70. He'd have to hit two in one game—something he was capable of doing but a feat that was always difficult. As usual, though, McGwire was up to the challenge.

He homered in the third inning for his 69th of the year. He walked his next time up but had another try in the seventh inning. The game was tied, 3–3, and the Cardinals had two runners on base with two out. Facing Montreal righthander Carl Pavano, McGwire lined his 70th home run of the season to left field.

It was a fitting ending to an incredible season. After the game, McGwire said of his feat, "It blows me away."[6]

As the 1999 season opened, fans eagerly awaited more exciting performances from McGwire.

He did not disappoint them, once again hitting mammoth home runs at an alarming rate. McGwire continued to set records and reach milestones that put him in the company with the best players ever. In August, he became only the sixteenth player to hit 500 career home runs, reaching that mark in fewer at bats than anyone else in history. He also was the first person to hit career home run number four hundred and five hundred in back-to-back seasons.

He blasted an amazing 65 homers in 1999, making him only the second player ever to hit at least 50 home runs in four different seasons. The other player is Babe Ruth. But McGwire has the distinction of being the only person to ever hit 50 or more home runs in four consecutive seasons.

Chapter Notes

Chapter 1. Number 62

1. "McGwire Refuses to Obsess over Missed Time," *Associated Press*, August 17, 1996, <http://galton.uchicago.edu/~curtis/McGwire/timelost.html>.

2. *Current Biography*, July 1988, p. 34.

Chapter 2. California Dreaming

1. Peter Gammons, "Here Come the Young Lions," *Sports Illustrated*, July 13, 1987, p. 42.

2. Dave Kindred, "A Man Among Children," *The Sporting News*, December 15, 1997, p. 19.

3. Mel Antonen, "The Mark McGwire Story," *USA Today*, May 10, 1996, p. 1C.

4. Kindred, p. 19.

5. Ibid.

6. Ron Fimrite, "The Bay Area Bombers," *Sports Illustrated*, April 4, 1988, p. 49.

7. Kit Stier, "Baseball's Newest Media Darling," *The Sporting News*, June 22, 1987, p. 10.

8. Fimrite, p. 49.

9. Joel Stein, "The Fun Is Back," *Time*, July 27, 1998, p. 45.

Chapter 3. College Years

1. Nancy Mazmanian, "Lines Finally Form for Mark McGwire," *Touchdown Illustrated*, November 19, 1983, p. 110.

2. Ibid.

3. Ron Fimrite, "The Bay Area Bombers," *Sports Illustrated*, April 4, 1988, p. 49.

4. Mike Eisenbath, "Bright Lights Not Big Mac's Chosen Style," *St. Louis Post-Dispatch*, August 10, 1997, p. 1F.

5. 1982 Official Alaska Central Baseball League statistics provided by the Anchorage Glacier Pilots.

6. Mazmanian, p. 110.

7. Danny Knobler, "McGwire Inspires Revival in USA Program," *Baseball America*, April 1, 1984, p. 30.

8. Kevin Modesti, "McGwire Leads Nation in Homers," *Herald* (USC Sports Information Office), April 10, 1984.

9. Knobler.

Chapter 4. New Challenges

1. Peter Richmond, "Olympic Team Takes Its Show on the Road," *Miami Herald*, July 14, 1984, p. 1C.

2. Dave Nightengale, "Going for the Major League Gold," *The Sporting News*, July 28, 1986, p. 6.

3. Peter Gammons, "Here Come the Young Lions," *Sports Illustrated*, July 13, 1987, p. 42.

4. "McGwire Leads Modesto's 4-Star Infield," *San Jose Mercury News*, July 18, 1985, p. 6G.

Chapter 5. Rookie Wonder

1. Kit Stier, "Baseball's Newest Media Darling," *The Sporting News*, June 22, 1987, p. 10.

2. *Current Biography*, July 1988, p. 35.

3. "McGwire Timeline," *CNN/Sports Illustrated Web Site*, <http://cnnsi.com/baseball/mlb/1998/target61/timeline/index.html>.

4. Tom Timmerman, "McGwire's Stature Rose as Tears Fell," *St. Louis Post-Dispatch*, September 20, 1997, p. 14.

Chapter 6. World Champs

1. Ron Kroichick, "Double Damage," *Sport*, October 1990, p. 109.

2. Ibid., p. 106.

3. Ibid., p. 111.

4. Kit Stier, "Breakup Doesn't Hurt McGwire's Play," *The Sporting News*, March 20, 1989, p. 38.

5. "McGwire: A Study in Preparation," *The Sporting News On-Line*, May 20, 1998, <http://www.sportingnews.com/baseball/articles/19980603/78614.html>.

6. Dave Nightengale, "Henderson Shoots Down Jays," *The Sporting News Baseball Guide, 1990 Edition*, p. 199.

Chapter 7. Downs and Ups

1. Mel Antonen, "The Mark McGwire Story," *USA Today*, May 10, 1996, p. 1C.

2. Mark McGwire (Interview by Peter Gammons of ESPN SportsCenter), <http://galton.uchicago.edu/~curtis/McGwire/gammonschat.html>.

3. Austin Murphy, "In Sight," *Sports Illustrated*, p. 34.

4. Ron Kroichick, "McGwire Finding '92 an Uplifting Season," *The Sporting News*, May 18, 1992, p. 13.

5. Antonen.

6. "McGwire Refuses to Obsess over Missed Time," *The Associated Press*, August 17, 1996, <http://galton.uchicago.edu/~curtis/McGwire/timelost.html>.

Chapter 8. Chasing History

1. "McGwire Refuses to Obsess over Missed Time," *The Associated Press*, August 17, 1996, <http://galton.uchicago.edu/~curtis/McGwire/timelost.html>.

2. Dave Kindred, "A Man Among Children," *The Sporting News*, December 15, 1997, p. 19.

3. "Putting His Money Where His Heart Is: McGwire Goes to Bat for Abused, Neglected Children," *Minneapolis Star Tribune*, June 11, 1998, p. 2C.

4. Steve Wulf, "Most Happy Fella," *Sports Illustrated*, June 1, 1992, p. 44.

5. William Ladson, "Bay Area Bambino," *Sport*, April 1997, p. 50.

6. "McGwire Blasts Two More on Final Day," *ESPN Sportszone*, <http://espnet.sportszone.com/ mlb/1998/980927/recap/monstl.html>.

Career Statistics

Year	Team	G	AB	R	H	2B	3B	HR	RBI	BB	Avg.
1986	Oakland	18	53	10	10	1	0	3	9	4	.189
1987	Oakland	151	557	97	161	28	4	49	118	71	.289
1988	Oakland	155	550	87	143	22	1	32	99	76	.260
1989	Oakland	143	490	74	113	17	0	33	95	83	.231
1990	Oakland	156	523	87	123	16	0	39	108	110	.235
1991	Oakland	154	483	62	97	22	0	22	75	93	.201
1992	Oakland	139	467	87	125	22	0	42	104	90	.268
1993	Oakland	27	84	16	28	6	0	9	24	21	.333
1994	Oakland	47	135	26	34	3	0	9	25	37	.252
1995	Oakland	104	317	75	87	13	0	39	90	88	.274
1996	Oakland	130	423	104	132	21	0	52	113	116	.312
1997	Oakland	105	366	48	104	24	0	34	81	58	.284
	St. Louis	51	174	38	44	3	0	24	42	43	.253
1998	St. Louis	155	509	130	152	21	0	70	147	162	.299
1999	St. Louis	153	542	118	145	21	1	65	147	133	.278
Totals		1,688	5,673	1,059	1,498	240	6	522	1,277	1,185	.265

G—Games
AB—At Bats
R—Runs
H—Hits
2B—Doubles

3B—Triples
HR—Home Runs
RBI—Runs Batted In
BB—Bases on Balls
Avg.—Batting Average

Where to Write
Mark McGwire

On the Internet at:

http://players.bigleaguers.com/Mark_McGwire.html

http://espn.sportszone.com/mlb/profiles/profile/3866.html

http://www.cnnsi.com/baseball/mlb/nl/players/Mark.McGwire

http://ww1.sportsline.com/u/baseball/mlb/players/3176.htm

http://www.stlcardinals.com

Index